DINO JOKE Book

by Terry Deary

Illustrated by Stuart Trotter

Hippo Books
Scholastic Children's Books
London

Scholastic Children's Books,
Scholastic Publications Ltd,
7-9 Pratt Street, London NW1 OAE

Scholastic Inc.,
730 Broadway, New York, NY 10003, USA

Scholastic Canada Ltd,
123 Newkirk Road, Richmond Hill,
Ontario, Canada L4C 3G5

Ashton Scholastic Pty Ltd,
P O Box 579, Gosford, New South Wales,
Australia

Ashton Scholastic Ltd,
Private Bag 1, Penrose, Auckland,
New Zealand

First published by Scholastic Children's Books 1992

Typeset by Contour Typesetters, Southall, London
Printed by Cox & Wyman

10 9 8 7 6 5 4 3 2 1

Contents

1
S'no Joke Being a Snowman

My story begins on a bitterly cold night. A blizzard of hailstones swept across the frozen Arctic wastes driven by a force nine gale. It was fifty-five below zero and the snow was two miles deep. Perfect weather, in fact.

My name is Freeze. They call me that because I'm so cool. And because, of course, I'm a snowball. The smartest, whitest snowball in the North. I'm sharp as an icicle and hard as hail.

I live at the Pole and I'm made out of snow, packed hard as ice. Guess you could call me a Pole-ice-man.

Let me tell you about the weirdest case I ever worked on. The case of the Unsmiling Snowman.

THIS SAD STORY IS NOT FOR THE TENDER HEARTED IT WILL HAVE YOU CRYING TILL THE TEARS RUN DOWN YOUR LEGS AND MAY GIVE YOU WATER ON THE KNEE.
YOU HAVE BEEN WARNED!
THE PUBLISHERS WILL NOT BE RESPONSIBLE!

It all began when the young snowman, Prince Chillibilli, fell in love with a snow girl. But why the hail am I telling you this? You've probably read the famous poem I wrote about the case. It's one of my best. Just in case you haven't read it, here it is . . .

S'NO JOKE BEING A SNOWMAN.

There once was a snowgirl quite small
And a snowman for her charms did fall.
He asked. "Any chance
Of us having a dance?"
She said, "Yes! Take me to the Snow Ball."

He said, "You're just like a white rose,
From the top of your head to your toes."
She said, "You're as nice
As a bucket of ice...
It's a pity about your red nose!"

He said "That's a carrot my chuck!"
The girl took a really hard look.
She said, "It's as flat
As a steam-rollered cat,
And it makes you look more like a duck."

Then like a fat white Cinderella
The snowgirl danced with her iced fella
He gave her a rose,
She gave him a nose,
He was happy 'cos now he could smell 'er.

The snowman (who was a big fool)!
Kissed the snowgirl on her cheek so cool.
Her face it did blush
With a burning hot flush,
And she turned to a slushy iced pool.

She went twice as soft as old butter,
The snowman he started to stutter,
"Oh, my d-d-dear
You are melted, I fear!"
And he watched her run off down the gutter.

The snowman was one sorry bloke.
His snow-heart was really quite broke.
With a heart-rending sigh
And a tear in his eye
He said "Being a snowman's no joke!"

And that was the start of Prince Chillibilli's misery. Nothing could make him smile. His dad, King Permafrost, almost melted his brain until, at last he came up with an idea . . .

REWARD.

TEN THOUSAND ICICLES, A FREE SUMMER HOLIDAY TO THE SOUTH POLE AND A NEW FRIDGE FOR THOSE WARM SUMMER EVENINGS.

ALL YOU HAVE TO DO IS MAKE PRINCE CHILLIBILLI SMILE!

SIGNED..... *King Permafrost*

They came from miles around to try. They failed. At last King Permafrost called in the polar police. The chief inspector sent me to the Ice Palace . . .

"This is a case for the Polar Police," His Majesty said. His eyes glittered like two lumps of black coal . . . probably because they *were* two lumps of black coal. "Spare no expense! Go the the ends of the earth! But find someone to bring a smile to Chillibilli's face!"

"Yes, your majesty," I said and slid out of the palace like a bobsleigh on a banana skin.

The trouble is, let's face it, snow people aren't very funny. I had to find people in the ice world who could make a snowball snigger or an ice cream scream.

I took the first iceberg to Tibet, home of the Yeti. As snowmen go they're pretty abominable . . . and their jokes aren't too good either. But it was a start.

2.
The Land of the Abominable Snow People

I knocked on the door to Tibet . . .

An abominable snowgirl let me in.

"Hello," she smiled. She had one tooth in the middle of her ugly face. As a snowball, of course, I can't stand central-eating! Her mouth was so wide she could have eaten a banana sideways. It was so wide she could have sung a duet with herself.

She had beautiful, white hair. It ran all down her back – none on her head, but a lot on her back.

"Hello, I'm Pole-ice Constable Freeze," I said. "Are you a yeti?"

"How did you know my name?" she gasped.

"Your name is Yeti?"

"No. My name is Betty. Sorry, I didn't hear you properly."

She had jelly in one ear and custard in the other. I guess that made her a trifle deaf.

We set off up the side of Everest, the world's tallest mountain, and she told me all about the region.

"This seems a romantic sort of place," I said.

"Ooh! It is!" she sighed and told me the tale.

THERE'S AN ANCIENT YETI LEGEND ABOUT A BOY YETI AND A GIRL YETI WHO ELOPED ONE MOONLIT NIGHT. THEY CLIMBED TO THE TOP OF THIS MOUNTAIN AND NEVER CAME BACK DOWN.

HOW ROMANTIC.

NOT REALLY THEY FELL OFF THE OTHER SIDE.

As I rolled up the side of Everest I started to turn green. "What's this?" I asked my Yeti guide.

"It's special Himalayan snow moss that only grows on the side of Everest."

"But why is it sticking to me?" I moaned and tried to scrape the stuff off.

"Because you have no feet. You are rolling up the hill like a stone," Betty explained. "As the ancient Yeti proverb goes, a rolling stone gathers snow moss."

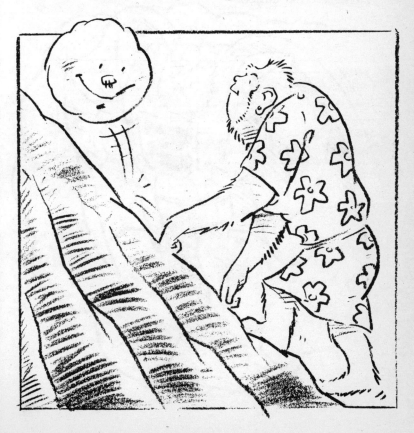

At last we reached the edge of the snow line and I felt more at home rolling over snow. Then I saw something that would have turned my heart as cold as ice . . . if it wasn't already. We passed a gigantic pair of shoes by the side of the road. If the feet that fitted them stepped on me then I'd be the thinnest pole-ice-man in the pole-ice force. "Whose are those shoes?" I gasped.

"They belong to Superyeti – the greatest hero ever born," she explained.

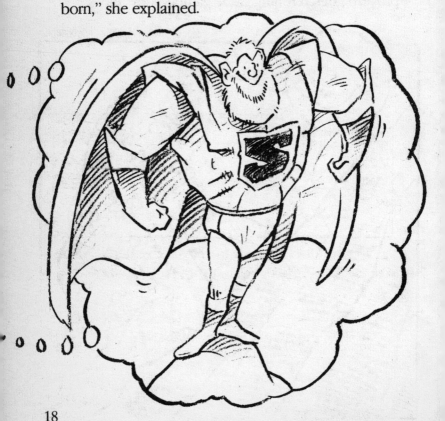

"But why does he need such huge shoes?" I asked.

"For his amazing feats, slush-brain! I even know where you can find giant snails!"

"Where?"

"On the ends of a giant's fingers, of course." Betty thought she was funny and laughed all the way up the mountain.

At last we reached a group of stone and turf huts.

"That's my house across the road," Betty pointed.

A herd of tame yak were tramping down the street. One kick from one of those hooves and I'd be an ex-snowball.

"They're making a lot of noise," I said.

"Yeah. They're yakkety yak."

"How am I ever going to cross?" I wailed. "Prince Chillibilli will never smile if I don't get back with a joke."

"There's a zebra crossing over there," Betty said.

"Well, I hope he has more luck than me," I grumbled.

Finally Betty picked me up and carried me across the road, pushing her way through the yak. She carried me into the one-roomed house. An old Abominable Snowman was asleep in the corner.

"Why has he got that ruler on his pillow?" I asked.

"He likes to know how long he's slept," Betty whispered.

I looked around the bare room. "Must get a bit boring at nights in these parts," I said.

"Oh, no!" Betty squealed. "We often go to the cinema!"

"What do you like?" I asked.

"Last night my dad took me to see *The Monster From the Pit.*"

"What did he look like?"

"Really gruesome. Slimy and ugly with green teeth and a bolt through his neck!"

"I can *see* what your dad looks like," I told her. "I meant the monster!"

"Ooh! You're not a nice man," she said with a nudge of an elbow like an ice-pick.

"No . . . but I am an ice man – so be careful with those elbows!"

"Ah! Dad's waking up," Betty said, smiling down at the old Yeti.

He yawned and stretched. Betty introduced us.

"You'll have to excuse Dad," she smiled. "He's stupid."

Her dad looked a little hurt. "Am I?"

"Ye-es!" she cried. "You once went to a mind-reader and she only charged you half price, remember? The kids on our street have a joke about Dad," she chuckled. "What do you call a flea in Mr Yeti's brain?"

"I don't know. What *do* you call a flea in Mr Yeti's brain?"

"A space invader!" Betty shrieked.

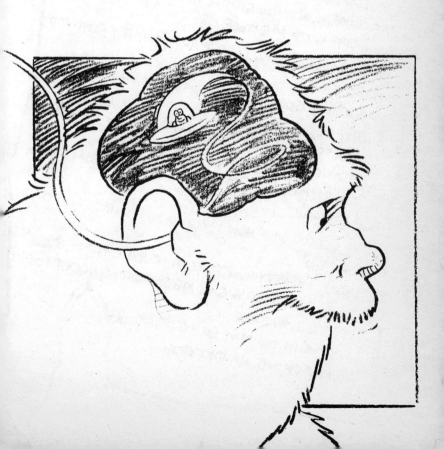

"Dad has a song. They call it the Yeti song . . . it goes like this!" and she sang it.

THE YETI SONG

I WENT OFF TO THE DOCTORS, THOUGH I WASN'T VERY ILL,
I DIDN'T WANT NO TABLET AND I DIDN'T WANT NO PILL.
I COULDN'T EAT ME DINNER 'COS SOME DIRTY ROTTEN THIEF
HAD CLIMBED IN THROUGH THE WINDOW AND HE'D
RUN OFF WITH ME TEEF.

ME TEEF WERE PEARLY WHITE AND HOW THEY GLITTERED
IN THE SUN.
I LOOKED SO GOOD MY HANDSOME FACE WAS LOVED BY
EVERYONE.
I HAD A SPARE SET IN THE DRAWER BUT THEY WERE
OLD AND MELLOW.
I TOOK THEM OUT AND THEY HAD TURNED A NASTY SHADE
OF YELLOW.

THE DOCTOR SAID "NOW, MY GOOD MAN WHAT CAN I DO
FOR YOU."
I SAID, "I'M VERY HUNGRY I CAN'T EVEN EAT MY STEW."
OH PLEASE PLEASE GIVE ME SOMETHING DOCTOR FOR
MY YELLOW TEEF."
AND WHAT DID THAT BRUTE GIVE TO ME?
A MATCHING HANDKERCHIEF.

"It's true," the old Yeti agreed. But he didn't seem to mind; in fact he seemed quite proud of the song.

"My dad's so daft he had rabbits tattooed on his bald head . . . he thought that from a distance they might look like hares."

"He's certainly balder than an egg," I agreed.

"I once bought Dad a comb for his birthday – he said he'd never part with it."

Mr Yeti just shook his head. "Better get off to work," he groaned.

"What sort of work do you do?" I asked.

"Dad's so ugly he makes a good living by hiring himself out to people with the hiccups. He wanted to be a clock maker . . . but he couldn't find the time."

"Has he had many jobs?"

"Well, he had a job in a fruit factory checking the fruit. He got the sack. He was throwing out all the bananas because they were bent."

"That's sad."

"Then he got a job raking leaves. Had to pack in when he had a nasty accident."

"What sort of accident could he have raking leaves?"

"He fell out of the tree.

Then he got a job as a lift operator. He got the sack because he kept getting lost."

The old Abominable Snowman lumbered out of the room. "Dad once taught me everything he knew," Betty sighed. "Those ten minutes of silence were unbearable."

"I'll never get a joke from him, then," I shrugged. "Guess I'll have to try the polar bears."

"Ahh!" Betty Yeti sniffed. "Lovely little cuddly white polar bears. I wish I could meet a polar bear."

"Lovely little cuddly white polar bears!" I spluttered. "They're only the most vicious things north of the South Pole! I'll be lucky to come out of the Arctic Circle in one piece. Still, I'm a pole-ice-man. And a snowball's gotta do what a snowball's gotta do!"

"Polar bears are lovely! Nothing as pretty as that can be really nasty. If they're as vicious as you say then how come polar bears have cuddly white coats?"

"Because they'd look pretty stupid in plastic macs!"

"I mean why are they big, white and fluffy?"

"Because if they were small, white and smooth they'd be aspirins!"

"Take me with you," Betty said shyly. "I'd protect you. And I may even find myself a boyfriend."

"Haven't you got one on Everest?" I asked.

"Not yeti," she admitted. "But if I travel the frozen wastes with you perhaps I'll find my Prince Charming."

"If we meet any short-sighted princes then I'll introduce you," I promised.

"Will you?" she asked.

"Yes. I'm a great romantic, just like you. I took my photographs to the chemist five years ago and they still haven't developed the film. I have the same dream as you."

"Yes. One day my prints will come," she smiled.

A romantic Yeti wasn't the best travelling companion in the world, but as a big bodyguard Betty seemed like a good idea.

We caught the first dog-sled to the Arctic Circle. It was pulled by huskies and the driver kept shouting "Mush!" I wished he wouldn't do that. If there's one word a snowball hates and fears it's "Mush".

We arrived at the door to the Arctic Circle in time for iced tea.

3.
The Land of the Polar Bear

The polar bear was huge. It reminded me of something my mother used to say when I was just a snowflake.

"What fur do you get from a polar bear?"

"I don't know, Mum. What fur do you get from a polar bear?"

"As fur away as possible, son! As fur away as possible."

But Betty Yeti wasn't scared. "Can you tell me the way to the nearest restaurant, my good man?" she asked.

The bear blinked and pointed a yellow claw to a wooden shed on the hill. We entered the restaurant. An even bigger bear stood behind the counter. There were friendly, welcoming signs on the wall behind him . . .

FORGIVE YOUR ENEMIES - BUT NEVER FORGET THEIR NAMES.

BEWARE OF MY DOG FROST REMEMBER FROST BITES!

I MAY HAVE MY FAULTS - BUT BEING WRONG ISN'T ONE OF THEM.

BIRDS OF A FEATHER THAT FLOCK TOGETHER MAKE A GOOD TARGET.

I looked around for the dog called Frost. I hate dogs.

"Where's the dog?" I asked.

"I don't let him in the restaurant," the polar bear snarled. "The dog has ticks."

"So, don't wind him up," I suggested.

"I mean he barks 'Tick-woof-tock-woof-tick-woof-tock-woof.'"

"Why does your dog go 'tick-woof-tock-woof-tick-woof-tock-woof?'"

"'Cos he's a watch-dog."

Betty's stomach was rumbling like an avalanche.

"How much for dinner?" she asked.

"Two pounds a head," the bear growled.

"Then I'll have a couple of heads and throw in a leg," Betty ordered.

"Can I see the menu?" I asked. When I'd read it I wished I hadn't. I didn't at all like the look of the Snowball Surprise!

And the rest of the menu was in the form of riddles:

Menu

It's yellow and stupid

Thick Custard.

It runs around Paris at noon, wrapped in a paper bag and crying, "The Bells! The Bells!"

The Lunch-pack of Notre Dame.

Legless spiders

Sultanas.

Bread on both sides and easily frightened

Chicken Sandwich.

A Central American at the North Pole

A Mexican Chilli.

Cheese that is made backwards

Edam.

Cat's Breakfast

Mice Crispies.

A pig running round with no clothes on

Streaky Bacon.

At least it was nice and cold in the restaurant. In fact, it was so cold even the potatoes kept their jackets on!

I fancied the iced strawberry milkshake but I wasn't too sure about this restaurant.

"Where do you get your milkshakes from?" I asked.

"From nervous cows."

"I'll have a hamburger, please."

"With pleasure."

"No, with ketchup. Will my hamburger be long?"

"No. It'll be round and flat."

The giant bear served us and I plucked up the courage to ask him, "Do you know a joke that would make Prince Chillibilli laugh?"

The bear frowned. "Yeah," he growled. "A salesman called round yesterday selling penguin-flavoured crisps. Now travelling salesmen know all the best jokes. Keeps their customers happy. Makes them buy more. Anyway, this travelling salesman, he said, 'What do you call a rich bear?'"

"I don't know. What do you call a rich bear?"

"Winnie the Pools!" He laughed. "Heh! Heh! Heh!"

"Don't you know any funny jokes?" Betty asked boldly.

The bear scowled at her and snarled. "No. But I do know a cure for your baldness. I'd stick your head in boiling water."

"Would that make my hair grow?"

"No, but it might shrink your head to fit the hair that you've got," he said and laughed cruelly as he wiped his claws on his apron.

"These Arctic polar bears are totally different from the black bears in Tibet," Betty sniffed.

"What's the difference between an Arctic polar bear and a Tibetan black bear?" I asked.

"Oh, about two continents and the Pacific Ocean," Betty said.

I ate my burger. "This is gristly," I complained.

"That's right. We eat grizzly bears when we can't get fresh supplies of penguins," the polar bear said. "Of course grizzly bears are stupid compared to us intelligent polar bears," he said. "We have a song about the grizzly bears – want to hear it?"

I didn't. I wanted to get off to find the joke that would make Prince Chillibilli smile. But the polar bear was big and fierce and I didn't want to upset him. "I'd love to hear your grizzly bear song," I lied. So he sang it.

THE GRIZZLY BEAR SONG

The grizzly bear loves honey, as everybody knows.
He'll eat it till it fills his face and covers up his nose.
He'll eat it till it drips right down and gunges up his
   toes.
The mess he makes! It's just as well he doesn't wear no
   clothes . . .
Isn't it?

So if you're eating honey and you see a bear go by,
You'd better hide it double quick or he will drool and
   sigh.
He'll plead and beg and ask for some, and maybe
   start to cry!
And if you tell him "no" then he may punch you in the
   eye . . .
Would you like that?

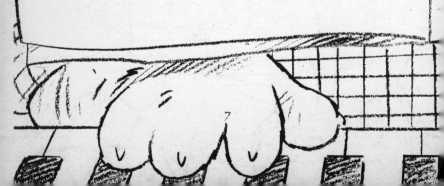

The bear is only happy with a pot of that sweet goo,
And if you want to keep your jar there's just one thing
to do:
Just tell the bear that you live in that town called
Timbuktu,
He'll go away for ever more and never bother you . . .
. . . Again.

Now why, you ask, would grizzly bears go search in
some place new?
Well, bears are good at reading, writing and at spelling
too.
They're *sure* there are no honey hives in that town I
told you.
Why's that? Because they know there's just one "B" in
Timbuktu!
. . . (But don't ever tell them you live in Brambleby
Road in Blackburn between Bury, Burnley, Bolton
and Bradford!)

All that talk about honey was making me hungry again.
I wondered if the bear could serve me my favourite.

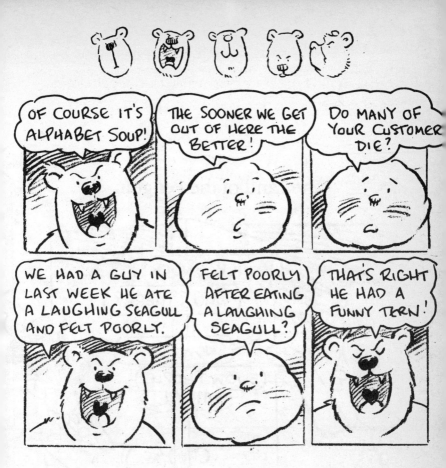

As we left, the waiter called after us, "If you want some real laughs you should see the penguins. Funny little guys. I have to laugh every time I eat one!"

"But the penguins are thousands of miles away in the Antarctic. I'd have to cross the equator to get there. I'd join the endangered PCs! I'd melt!"

"Not if you go to the zoo, stupid," the bear sneered. We went to the zoo.

4.
The Land of the Penguin

"Sorry to keep you waiting," the zoo-keeper said, "I've been looking after a sick bird."

"What can you do for a sick bird?" I asked.

"Oh, you can give it tweetment," the man explained.

"Can we see the penguins?" Betty asked.

The zoo-keeper shook his head sadly.

"We had a very nasty accident last week," he said. "Some vicious kids broke into the zoo one night. Took all the penguins and threw them to the polar bears."

"Oooh!" Betty squealed. "Did the polar bears eat them?"

"No," the man smiled. "They couldn't get the wrappers off."

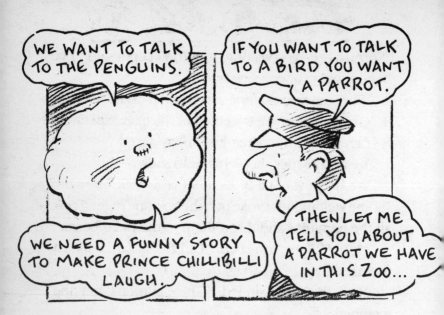

He used to belong to the captain of a ship. It was a cruise ship. Every night after dinner the passengers would have an entertainer. One night it was a magician. The parrot sat on his perch and watched the magician closely. Every time the magician tried a trick the parrot would cry out and give the game away. When he had a card up his sleeve the parrot would cry. . .

When he had a rabbit hidden down his trousers the parrot would cry . . .

The magician was furious, but he couldn't gag the parrot because it was the captain's favourite. Then, one night, the ship hit an iceberg and sank like a stone. The magician swam for it and managed to find an empty raft. What should be perched on the end of the raft? That's right! The parrot. The parrot stared with his little black eyes as the magician collapsed on the raft. When morning came the magician opened his eyes. The parrot spoke at last . . .

The zoo-keeper shuffled off, laughing at his own story. We followed the signs to the penguin pool.

"I once had a friend who was a magician," Betty said. "He promised to saw me in half one day. I told him to go off and practise on his family."

"Did he have a large family?"

"He had lots of half-sisters and brothers," she said.

When we reached the penguin pool we introduced ourselves to the biggest penguin who squawked, "Pleased to meet you. My name's Peregrine. Peregrine Penguin."

"Pleased to meet you, Peregrine," I said. "Know any good jokes?"

"We know a million!" Peregrine Penguin promised. "What bird sounds like a train?" he began.

"I don't know. What bird sounds like a train?"

"A Puffin!

What goes 'Boo-hoo!
Boo-hoo! Splatt! Splatt!'?"
he went on.

"I don't know. What
goes 'Boo-hoo! Boo-hoo!
Splatt! Splat!'?"

"The zoo-keeper crying
his eyes out!"

"Why was he crying his
eyes out?"

"He was trying to wash
his front doorstep . . . and he
broke his washing machine!"

"That's not kind," Betty
Yeti said.

"Hey! Do you know why
he wears rubber gloves
when he feeds the seals?"

"No. Why does he wear
rubber gloves when he
feeds the seals?"

"So his nails won't go
rusty!"

The penguin waved a flipper at his friends.

HEY! MATES, THIS SNOWBALL IS COLLECTING JOKES FOR PRINCE CHILLIBILL!

TELL HIM WHY THE THREE MUSKATEERS TRAVELLED WITH A PENGUIN.

THAT'S BECAUSE THE PENGUIN'S MIGHTIER THAN THE SWORD

A penguin waddled up to me and pecked me sharply. "Did you hear about the time a penguin went to the doctor?" he asked. "She asked the doctor if he had anything for chapped beaks. The doctor gave her some lip salve. He asked if she wanted to pay for it. She said, 'No. Put it on my bill!'"

An old penguin pushed a piece of paper into my hand. "Here's a page from the *Penguin Book of Jokes*.

- What do you get if you cross a skunk with a hedgehog?
  A PORCUPONG.
- What do you get if you cross the Atlantic Ocean with the SS. Titanic?
  HALF WAY.
- What do you get if you cross a tiny flying insect with a camel?
  A HUMPED BACK MIDGE.
- What do you get if you cross a snake and a magic spell?
  AN ADDERCADABRA... OR ABRADACOBRA.
- What do you get if you cross Concorde with a tube of Super-Glue?
  SOMETHING THAT BREAKS THE SOUND BARRIER THEN MENDS IT AGAIN.

Another penguin showed me his collection of Penguin Books . . .

KEEPING DRY IN A STORM. BY ANNA RACK.

POLAR WEATHER. BY I.C. BLASTS.

HUNGRY PENGUIN M.T. GUTTS.

LOOKING AFTER PENGUINS. BY SUE KREPER

THE VANISHING FISH. BY HENRIETTA LOTT

THE GREAT ZOO ESCAPE BY FREDA LOTTOVEM

THE DEATH FUNNY PENGUIN. BY PERCY VERE

THE GHOSTLY PENGUIN. BY DENISE R. KNOCKIN' + TERRY FYDE.

PENGUINS COOKBOOK. BY ANN OVEN

THE PENGUIN DIETBOOK. BY WILMA CLOTHESFITT

"We have more chance of getting a laugh from a reindeer!" I sighed. We walked back towards the entrance.

"Hey!" a penguin screeched. "That's illegal!" I stopped.

"What's illegal?"

"A sick bird of prey!"

The zoo-keeper stopped us. "Before you go, let me tell you the tragic tale of the man who came in here last week."

"Go ahead," Betty urged.

I guess I should have stayed to check out that story of the mad motorist. But pole-ice work came second to the task of making the prince smile.

We went to Lapland.

5.
The Land of the Reindeer

Reindeer are the meanest animals in the
Arctic Circle. The one who met us was
so mean he had a burglar alarm on
his dustbin.

Betty gave me a peculiar look. "Sometimes I think
you're as daft as my dad."

"If I thought I was as daft as your dad I'd bash my
head against that cliff!"

"If you were as daft as my dad you'd probably miss,"
she smiled. She turned back to the reindeer and spoke
in her politest voice.

"Please can you help us out?" Betty Yeti asked.

"Yep. Which way did you come in?" the reindeer snapped.

"I mean we want to hire a sledge," I explained.

"Everyone knows how to hire a sledge."

"How do you hire a sledge?"

"Put a couple of bricks under the runners!" the deer drawled.

"We want to get to the top of that mountain," I said.

"I'll take you in the lift," he offered.

We climbed into the cable car and whirred up to the top of the mountain.

We stepped out into Reindeer Town. "I'll have to leave you here," the reindeer sighed. "I'm banned from reindeer town."

"Why are you banned?"

"Rudolph and Prancer and Dancer were caught smoking in their stables," he sighed.

"If Rudolph and Prancer and Dancer were smoking, then how come *you* were banned."

He shook his antlers. "It was me that set fire to them," he said.

We set off down the main street and came to a huge stone building. A sign outside said THE TOMB OF GRIEG.

"Who's Grieg?" Betty asked.

An old reindeer stood at the door. "Come in and see," he said.

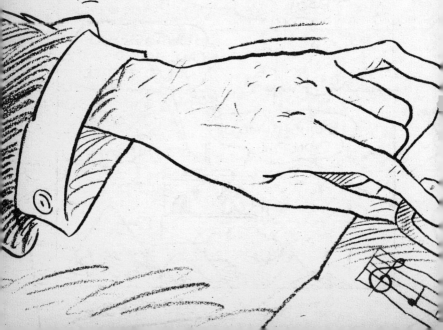

We walked into the dark, cool building and he told us the story.

"Grieg was the greatest composer who ever lived in Norway! When he died they brought him to the top of this mountain and put him in this glass coffin so everyone could see him. It's so cold they thought it might preserve the body."

We looked into the glass coffin in the middle of the building. A white-haired old man lay there. Beside his hand was a pile of music. "That's a copy of all the music he ever composed," the reindeer said.

As we watched the wrinkled old hand began to move.

"Eek!" Betty squeaked.

The hand reached across and picked up a rubber. Slowly it brought the rubber back and began to drag it across the pages of music. One by one the notes disappeared.

I groaned and asked, "Don't the reindeer have any favourite jokes?"

The old reindeer scratched his antler and thought. "They have a good laugh at the helicopter that flies up the mountain from the valley."

"What's funny about a helicopter?" Betty Yeti asked.

"It wobbles," he said.

"What do you call this wobbling helicopter?" I asked.

"A jellicopter, of course!" he hooted.

I sighed. "Do you know any other jokes?" I asked.

"I do . . . but it'll cost you a hundred pounds."

"That's mean," I said.

The reindeer nodded. "I know. It's in the blood. Reindeers are so mean. Do you want to know how mean reindeer are?"

"Tell me."

"How do mean reindeer keep warm when it's cold?"

"I don't know. How do mean reindeer keep warm when it's cold?"

"They sit around a candle."

"That's mean."

"And that's nothing! When it gets *really* cold they light it!"

"Aren't there any generous reindeer?"

"Oh, you come across them once in a blue moose."

"Look," I said. "Don't you know any really funny creatures in the Arctic Circle?"

"Lemmings are funny," he said. "Every year they rush to the cliffs and throw themselves into the rivers and drown. You have to be pretty funny in the head to do that," he said.

"I don't know," Betty said. "It reminds me of a story about a family that drove their car over a cliff . . ." And as we set off for Lemming Land Betty told me the tale . . .

A FAMILY WENT OUT IN THEIR CAR FOR THE DAY
BUT THEY DROVE OFF A CLIFF AND SANK IN THE BAY.
THE LIFEGUARD SAILED OUT PICKED THEM UP AND HE SAID
"WITHOUT DOUBT THE POOR FAMILY ARE ALL OF THEM DEAD!"

STILL THEY SENT FOR A DOCTOR WITH OINTMENTS AND PILLS
HE SAID THAT HE KNEW THEM. "A FAMILY CALLED HILL!
YOUNG JOHNNY AND SALLY WITH THEIR MUM AND THEIR DAD.
THEY'VE ALL GONE TOGETHER A PITY HOW SAD."

But a passing young man from an opera show
Said "What? Can't you cure them? Let me have a go!"
And he started to sing every song that he knew
Like "Over the Rainbow" and "Love, love me do"

And as he was singing to general surprise
Young Johnny sat up and he rubbed at his eyes.
Then Sally came round then her mum and her dad!
They all looked as lively as ever they had.

The doctor was gobsmacked the lifegaurd as well
They said. "How did you do that? Some magic? Please
   tell".
The singer said "Goodness me this is no trick!
The hills are alive with the sound of music!"

6.
The Land of the Lemming

The street was teeming with little animals running every which way. They all looked pretty miserable. One was selling fridges.

Betty Yeti pointed out a water-skiing shop. "He should be happy with business," she said. "Do you do much trade in water-skis for lemmings?" she asked the little, furry, yellow creature. "There are lots of lakes around here."

He shook his head sadly. "They're no use for skiing on," he shrugged. "Not *one* of the lakes has a slope on it!"

"Of course you'll have heard about the rich lemming. He was so happy he decided not to join his friends in jumping over the cliff. He went out and bought a horse from a farmer. The farmer said the horse was a bit unusual. It only knew two commands.

"'If you want it to go you have to say FEW and if you want it to stop then say AMEN.'

"The lemming thought this was a bit odd, but he was a very rich lemming so he bought the horse anyway. The next morning he took it out for a ride. '*FEW* !' he cried and the horse set off. It started to trot, then it started to canter, then it started to gallop. The rich lemming realised that it was heading straight for the cliffs. 'Help!' he cried. 'I've forgotten the word to stop him!'

"The horse went faster and faster and nearer and nearer to the cliff. 'This is it! The end! Oh Lord,' he prayed, 'Save my soul! AMEN!'

"And as he said AMEN the horse stopped a whisker short of the cliff edge. The rich lemming opened his eyes and saw how close he was to joining the lemmings tumbling over the cliff. He wiped the sweat off his brow with the back of his paw and said, '*PHEW* ! That was a close a-a-a-a-ghh!'"

AAAAAG

"Another friend, Arthur, jumped in the river to stop a fight."

"That was brave. Who was fighting?"

"Arthur and a polar bear."

"Have any of your friends drowned, the way lemmings are supposed to?" Betty Yeti asked.

"Larry Lemming drowned when he was playing football."

"How can you drown playing football?"

"The manager flooded the pitch."

"Why did the manager flood the pitch?"

"Because he wanted to bring on the sub!"

"I miss old Larry, he couldn't play football but he was a good friend. I'd just bought the team a lighter... that was 'cos they kept losing their matches."

"Are you going to jump?"

"If I don't get better soon."

"Are you ill?"

"I went to the doctor's," the lemming said.

I looked at the poor lemming. "I think you're suffering from hypochondria," I said.

He nodded sadly. "Probably. I've got every other illness."

"Aren't there any happy lemmings?" I asked.

"Funny you should ask that. There was once a happy lemming. Pull up that icicle, sit down and I'll tell you about him."

We sat on the icicle. It was beautifully cold. The lemming began his story.

"Once upon a time twin lemmings were born. One baby lemming was always miserable, always crying and always moaning . . . just like a good little lemming should. But the other baby lemming was very odd. It was always laughing, always smiling and always content.

"When the weather was too bad to go out to play the sad lemming moaned and groaned because it was bored; but the happy lemming was cheerful and said, 'Never mind, the rain will help the flowers to grow.'

"As the twins grew up the happy lemming grew worse! When times were bad and the family went hungry the sad lemming moaned. 'Oooh! I'm so hungry, I'm the world's most unhappy lemming!'

"But the happy lemming chuckled, 'Never mind. We were getting a bit too fat anyway. This diet will do us good!'

"The daddy lemming and the mummy lemming were very worried. 'What are we going to do about our happy child?' they sighed. 'Life is cruel and life is hard. He'll have to find this out. You just can't go around being happy all the time!'

"So they went to the doctor.

"The doctor agreed. The happy lemming needed a short, sharp, nasty shock to stop his happy nonsense. 'Christmas is coming,' the wise old doctor said. 'Give the sad twin every toy he has ever wanted. Give the happy lemming an empty Christmas stocking. That will teach him not to be so foolish.'

"So, on Christmas Eve, Daddy Lemming and Mummy Lemming hung up the stockings in the young lemmings' rooms. The stocking for the sad lemming was packed with toys. The stocking for the happy lemming was empty. The parents looked at the empty stocking and agreed it just wasn't good enough.

"So, Daddy Lemming set off down the garden, crossed the garden fence and climed into the field where some horses lived. (The happy little lemming loved those horses and always wanted to ride a pony of his own). Daddy Lemming took the stocking and filled it full of the horses' manure and took it back to the house. He hung the stocking full of manure on the end of the bed of the happy lemming and went off to bed.

"Next morning there were cries of happiness from one room and cries of sadness from the other. Daddy Lemming and Mummy Lemming rushed into the room of the sad lemming. He was wailing and crying over his toys. 'This one's broken (sob) . . . I never wanted one of these (sob) . . . I hate the colour of this (sob) . . . this toy has no batteries (sob-sob-sob).'

"But in the other room the happy lemming was screaming with joy. He was up to his elbows in the horse manure, throwing it all around the room and laughing. 'Yippee!' he was crying. 'Father Christmas has left me a pony! I just haven't found it yet!'"

The lemmings were sadder than the Prince himself. I decided to head off home with my stories. I stood up and shook hands with the lemming.

"I hope you get better soon," I smiled.

He shook his pointy little head sadly. "No. I'm just off to buy myself a plastic coffin."

"Why would anyone want a plastic coffin?" Betty asked.

"For a vinyl resting place," he said.

There weren't a lot of laughs in Lemming Land.

Before we left, Betty stopped at a lemming chemist shop.

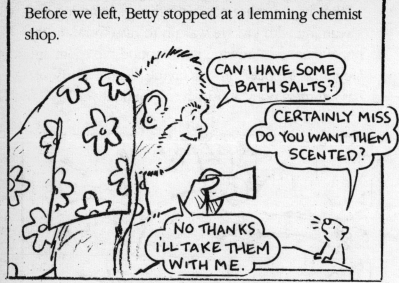

CAN I HAVE SOME BATH SALTS?

CERTAINLY MISS DO YOU WANT THEM SCENTED?

NO THANKS I'LL TAKE THEM WITH ME.

"Maybe the lemmings jump in the water for fun!" I said. "If we go to the seaside we may find a few laughs."

On the way I turned into my Pole-ice radio for the latest news . . .

A ship carrying a cargo of yo-yos has hit an iceberg – so far it has sunk 37 times.

A gang of thieves has raided the Greenland Zoo and set free 100 hares – police are combing the area.

A daffodil smuggler tried to get 200 bulbs out of Holland by swallowing them – he is now in prison and police say he will be out in the spring.

A runaway truck was last seen hurtling down a motorway at 100 mph, making rude noises at other cars – police have asked motorists to report sightings of this jugger-naughty.

A daring thief broke into a house and stole the kitchen sink – witnesses said he got clean away.

A cat has gone missing from its home in Greenland – it was last seen heading towards the hospital where it is hoping to become a first-aid Kit.

Mr Reader, the local newsagent, went to open his paper shop this morning only to find it had blown away.

Be on the lookout for the astronomer, I.C. Starrs, who got out of jail last night using his tel-escape.

Finally a reminder to all bears called Edward who are working outdoors – take your shovels but do not take your picks! I repeat – do not take your picks! We have information that today's the day the teddy bears have their picks nicked!

So much crime for me to crack! But first I had to find the joke that would crack Chillibilli's face with a smile.

So, we set off for the sea.

7.
The World of Water

The sand was very wet.

"Why is this sand wet?" I asked.

"Maybe the sea weed," Betty Yeti suggested.

"I like fish," I said. "I don't suppose you get much fish on Everest."

"Just in the chip shop," Betty told me.

"There's a chip shop on Mount Everest?" I asked.

"Yeah! It's a really exciting place. Last week there was a fight there."

"Anybody hurt?"

"Well, a couple of fish got battered."

"What made these yellow footprints on the sand?"

"Probably a lemon sole."

"Why is the sea roaring like that?"

"You'd roar if you had crabs in your bed!"

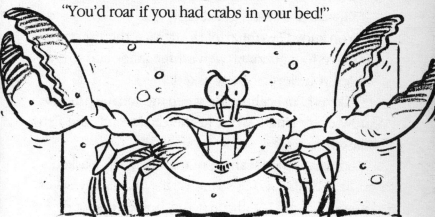

Suddenly something appeared on the surface. "There's something green and prickly out there," I said.

"What could be green and prickly?" Betty asked.

"A seasick hedgehog," I said.

"No, it's a flock of fish!" Betty cried.

"It's not a *flock*! It's a school. An underwater school!" I explained.

"*My* school may as well have been underwater," she sighed, "'cos all my marks were below 'C' level."

A fish popped its head over the surface. "What have you learned in school today?" I asked.

"Guzzintas," the fish said.

"Guzzintas? What's guzzintas?"

"You know! Two guzzinta four twice, three guzzinta six twice, four guzzinta twelve three times, and so on."

"Are you clever?" Betty asked.

"Clever? I'm brilliant! Between me and my sister we know every single word in the dictionary!" the fish boasted.

"So what's the meaning of meritocratic?" I asked.

"Er . . . ah . . .that's one of the words my sister knows!" he said. "Will you do my homework for me?"

the fish asked.

"That wouldn't be right," I told him.

"Maybe not . . . but at least you could try! I need to know the answer to the question, Why did Henry the Eighth have so many wives?"

"Easy," Betty said. "Because he liked to chop and change."

"So, can you tell me, how many sheep does it take to make a sweater?"

I shrugged. "I didn't even know that sheep could knit!"

"Maybe you could check my exam paper," the fish suggested.

"How on earth do you write under water?" Betty Yeti asked.

"Use a ball-point pen-guin of course!"

The fish handed me his test paper. I didn't reckon much on his chances of passing when I read it . . .

EXAM PAPER

GEOGRAPHY: Where is Yarmouth?

Same place as yours -
Under my nose.

GEOGRAPHY: What do you know about the Dead Sea?

I didn't know it was ill.

SCIENCE: What do you get hanging from Banana Trees?

Tired arms.

SCIENCE: Why do giraffes have long legs and long necks?

In case their feet smell.

SCIENCE: Describe an octopus.

An eight sided cat.

P.E.: You have a referee in football and an umpire in cricket, what do you have in bowls?
Gold fish.

GENERAL KNOWLEDGE: What are "Engineers"?
They're what an engine listens with.

HISTORY: When was the Iron Age?
Before drip-dry shirts were invented.

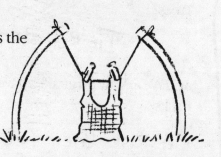

ENGLISH: Use the word "denial" in a sentence.
Denial is a river in Egypt.

GENERAL KNOWLEDGE: Why were the Middle Ages called the Dark Ages?
Because there were so many knights in them.

HISTORY: On what date did Columbus cross the Atlantic?

He didn't cross it on a date - he crossed it on a boat.

GENERAL KNOWLEDGE:
What is a biplane?

The last words a pilot says before he bails out.

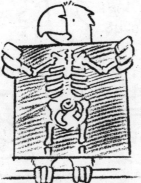

ENGLISH: Use the word "politics" in a sentence.

The parrot swallowed a watch so now politics.

HISTORY: Who found America?

I didn't know it was lost.

ENGLISH: Use the word "allocate" in a sentence.

Every time I see my friend Catherine I say "Allocate".

HISTORY: What happened to Boudicca after her last battle?

Julius Seized'er.

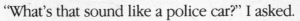

"What's that sound like a police car?" I asked.

"Ah! That'll be the underwater cops trying to catch me playing truant!"

"Do the underwater police have vehicles?"

"Of course! You never heard of a squid car? Ta-ta!" and the fish swam away.

"Time's running out," I said, "we must get back to the Ice-Palace. Maybe one of these jokes will make Chillibilli laugh."

And so we set off for Snow Land

"I suppose we could always cross the Arctic Ocean with a hyena," Betty said.

"What would that give us?"

"Waves of laughter, perhaps."

8.
The Land of the Snow People

It was good to be home in Snow Land. The snowman who opened the gate was wearing ten balaclava helmets. "That's to keep him cold," I explained to Betty Yeti.

"What do you call him?" she asked.

"You can call him anything you like. With ten balaclava helmets on he'll never hear you!"

At last we reached the palace.

"Come in! Come in!" King Permafrost said. "Tell me, Freeze, have you found anything to make Prince Chillibilli laugh?"

I was just about to tell him about my failure when the Prince himself called me over. "Freeze! Freeze! Who's that beautiful girl that just walked in with you?"

"Beautiful girl? You mean Betty Yeti?"

"She looks like a million dollars!"

He was right there. She was all green and crinkly.

"Oooh!" the Prince gurgled. "She just rolled her eyes at me!"

"Well, just roll them back to her," I told him.

"I'm so shy I don't know how to talk to a beautiful Yeti," the Prince confessed. "Can't you give me one of your famous songs?" he pleaded.

I scribbled a song about Betty Yeti's beauty on the back of a paper handkerchief . . . of course it was a tissue of lies. But Chillibilli seemed to like it. He picked up a small trumpet – all snowmen like a nice cornet – and began to play.

CHILLIBILLI'S LOVE SONG

Your eyes are the eyes of a woman in love,
Your face is beyond all compare.
Your lips are as soft as the wings of a dove . . .
But, gawd, what have you done to your hair?

You're as lovely as snow clouds – and nearly as clever,
I'm happy as I've ever felt.
I guess I could love you forever and ever . . .
Or at least till the day that I melt.

When you are my bride you'll be lovely in white,
At the church you will be a big hit.
The dressmakers here will work both day and night
To find you a dress that will fit.

So marry me now and a princess you'll be.
Your life will be filled up with riches.
(or maybe it will when my dad lends to me
Enough cash for a trip to the pictures.)

There was an excitement in the air like it was electric. But I knew it couldn't be electric – King Permafrost hadn't paid the bill.

"Introduce us," Prince Chillibilli ordered.

I introduced them. Their eyes met.

He kissed her. Their teeth met. It was love at first bite.

"I'd like to run my fingers through your hair," he said. "Can you remember where you left it?"

I tried to interrupt so I could get back to the business of making him laugh . . . and winning the prize. "Now, about these jokes, Your Highness . . ."

"Go away, Freeze," he said.

"But I want to make you laugh and get the reward," I cried.

"Go away, Freeze," Betty sighed.

"Why should I?"

92

Betty looked adoringly into her prince's charming eyes. "Because two's company," she said, "But Freeze a crowd."

"Hey! Hey! Hey!" Prince Chillibilli laughed. "That's really funny! Give Betty the prize . . . we'll take the trip to the South Pole as a honeymoon! Hey! Hey! Hey! Freeze a crowd! – I like it!"

I didn't. In fact it wasn't funny at all.

Like my mother always said, "It's hard to be a snowball. In fact it . . ."

S'NO JOKE!

I didn't get the prize but at least I got an invitation to the wedding. And King Permafrost invited me to be the Poet Laureate of Snow Land. That meant I had to write a poem to celebrate the occasion.

THE WEDDING OF CHILLI AND BETTY

An Abominable Snowgirl called Betty
Had sworn that a prince she would get. He
Could not fight her charms
As he danced in her arms.
When he asked "can we marry?" she let he.
Young Chilli he married the Yeti.
The Snow Prince would quite soon forget he
had once worn a Frown
For a girl who'd run down
An old drain like a string of spaghetti
The prince found the secret of laughter
Was hearing daft jokes and some dafter.
Now the couple they smile
Almost all of the while
As they happily live ever after.